Positive Discipline

Positive Discipline

Avery Nightingale

CONTENTS

First Printing, 2024

1 Introduction

Some family structures enable a safe, nurturing and interactive environment for young children to mature. Others offer less than favorable conditions for advocacy and empowerment of the adult(s) in their often desperate times. Positive Discipline techniques not only guide parents, caregivers, and educators how to stop undesirable behaviors in the young child but help the adult model or teach the child self-control, honor, and respect for self, others, and our world. During the first years of a child's life, the opportunity for a positive outcome of guidance is far more rewarding than always seeking to be punishing. As the adult assists the child in developing emotional regulation, the source of much early challenging behavior, the heart of a child is allowed to open and be filled with love, development, and learning.

Positive discipline is the practice of empowering parents (and educators) by giving simple and effective skills to use to guide their children.

2

Understanding Positive Discipline

The Positive Discipline model is put together with the final aim of inspiring capable, courageous citizens—people who have the skills to embrace their own abilities, tackle their own attempts, and make a vital contribution to their society. Positive ways to interact with your children involve really good interactions in an approach that really encourages potential instead of rebelling. It is a psychology that emphasizes the validity of the person: their strengths and weaknesses, their hopes and desires. There are two main components included in Nelsen's Positive Discipline model: Relationships (Respect and Connect) and the four integral parts of Positive Discipline (Validate, Understand, Assign, and Give Encouragement).

Positive Discipline utilizes the idea of using kindness and firmness simultaneously. It encourages parents to assist their child when they are performing well, while encouraging the development of practical and social skills that foster a deeper connection with their child. At the same time, it demands that parents take a no-nonsense or firm look at actions that involve chores or responsibilities and assign them accordingly. The idea of Positive Discipline is to shift the quiet respect from the parents to the children to a connection between their parents and to have them become aware of the consequences of their actions and then address them as a character-building opportunity. With its roots in research from Alfred Adler and Rudolph Dreikurs, Positive Discipline was established by Jane Nelsen and Lynn Lott in 1981 to support parents and other specialists understand and learn how to teach others the concepts developed by Alfred Adler to bring about a form of connection, dignity, and joy.

3

The Importance of Love in Shaping Behavior

Respect encourages students to partner with the teacher, creating a united front and avoiding harsh discipline measures. To respect is to "demonstrate high regard and genuine concern for [students'] well-being". "Positive discipline is guided by our respect for... each child". Corrective measures must reflect love and respect and help build mutual respect. Children are supremely attuned to the attitudes of those around them; if they do not feel love and respect, it is difficult for them to adopt love and respect for the adults in their lives. Lists the guidelines developed by the Committee for Children to support positive discipline; many of them center on demonstrating love and respect (Table 1). Likewise, the Love and Logic approach encourages love, respect, and logical consequences as important in promoting a positive and lasting behavioral change in students.

"Positive discipline is based on love and respect". Positive discipline reminds teachers to remain objective and to approach students with dignity and love, even in difficult situations. Love and respect are the fundamental underpinnings of behavior shaping. Love says "I care about you and I want you to learn. I believe in your abilities and I'm excited to see you succeed. I am committed to teach you self-discipline." Love builds relationships and strengthens self-esteem. Research supports the idea that "children thrive when they interact with warm adults who support them and watch out for their best interests".

4

Creating a Positive Environment

With a little effort, you can quickly get to a good point. Try to maintain a positive feel as long as you can. After all, it costs you nothing. Talk to your children respectfully. As strange as it may sound, children should never argue or talk about parents; adults argue and quarrel with one another. After reading this article, you may wonder where you can find the strength to create a positive atmosphere when it's hard, given all the challenges you face in today's world. The strength will be there. It can be found in your concern for the child. Children are prisoners at your concentration camp, innocent and unarmed. Being in place, they have no one to protect them but us adults. A negative atmosphere is a tool of power and is used in bargaining. By creating a positive atmosphere, we voluntarily refuse unnecessary inflicting pain on our children in order to gain your trust and love. If you successfully create a positive atmosphere, children will be glad to respond with good behavior, and any conversation about power used against them will become irrelevant.

When creating a loving and encouraging environment, your child is likely to respond with more positive behavior. If you're negative too, your child is not likely to be sweet and thoughtful. If you approach her with love, kindness, and patience, I promise your efforts will pay off. The more love you give, the more your child will be able to accept, and the more likely she will grow up to give love in return. Remember, as corny as it sounds, what goes around really does come around! Give love and patience, especially when your child doesn't appear to deserve them. When you follow your positive discipline plan, your child will come around and behave more appropriately. Think of a positive atmosphere as sunshine: Offer it with mild presence and your child will eventually feel warmth in response.

5

Setting Clear Expectations

Exchanging the word "to behave" for "to progress" reminds us to always seek the real, deep changes that are required to shape behaviors by sharing love and respect.

The discipline of shaping behavior with love allows us to make our life easier and more fun each day. Many of you have probably already noticed how practice gives the self-control necessary to use love as a strategy. It puts everybody on the same team, interested in the good of the group, and the distances between parental victories and what makes children happy decrease and disappear. We see the opportunity to be in each other's company that doesn't arise when we treat different activities as adversarial. While so much part of the process becomes natural to us, it becomes more difficult to return to the old track and want the aggressiveness of competition and frustration back.

Managing behavior is all about setting clear expectations and learning to identify opportunities to bring everyone closer. Truly, this becomes impossible if our only expectation is "to not mess things up." We have to remember that our relationship with our children matters at least as much as any simple task, and everyone wants to have good relations with their siblings. On the other hand, we don't wake up every day thinking about the possibility of "messing it all up and stirring up unnecessary fights." So hoping that our children will think about all day and decide to act that way gets in the way of necessary flexibility: a trait required to support our children's development.

6

Using Positive Reinforcement

Unlike those who choose Learning Models, Behavioral Reinforcement, or Human Cybernetic Educational Methods, who have no identifiable base unit for behavior change about which any verifiable claims can be made, anyone with curiosity enough to ask employs the Multiple Aspects of the Behavior in the System for Reinforcement Paradigm intimate to Reinf-Mostetic and One Thing Awareness Human Cybernetics. Instance of desired behaviors produce outcomes that can be much loved and are specifically intended that the person, animal, or robot interprets as such, for with dynamic reinforcement changes in behavior occur in real time. Everyone is already doing this, chit-chatting away, counseling and encouraging each other in myriad ways large and small to lost and found. With the additional humaneness of this behavioral referring to the only aspect of everyone we can be certain is there, the most humane, the most-ever-Proximal ourselves, our kind and wise Springer-Verlag book, Communicating Therapeutic Change Through Humanistic Health Methods, Seventhe Specific, revolves with ease abundantly positive reinforcement is safely available.

After punitive praise, let's break with tradition and move into the empirically based zone of positive reinforcement. This method of shaping behavior was developed by the great B. F. Skinner in the 1950s. Using his "operant conditioning model of learning" - the same model of reinforcement that has been fine-tuned and sanitized into Skinner's trademarked handout model that is known as the Castlefield Program in schools - we can get the learning behaviors of desired behavior change right. Of course, true to the "methods of yesterday go, the behaviors are shaped and reinforced by love instead of punishment, fear or avoidance techniques. And true to modernity, we consider multiple aspects of the distributed nervous system by engaging them all as opposed to getting brainy about neurotransmitters and receptors. The OTA learning model that we use in chapter 5, the standard "method of instruction" within Human Cybernetics itself, is its equal in all things pragmatic and expedient.

7

Teaching Problem-Solving Skills

This is how it works: You have a problem in academics in question. So, you first state the problem in detail – 'It takes me too long to do my homework, especially the math part.' When you go into detail, you already have so much knowledge on what is going wrong. What this step entails is describing your problem clearly. After you have described your problem and the reasons for it, the next step is to come up with a variety of possible solutions. So, don't try to hurry and fix the problem, just focus on coming up with as many ideas as you possibly can. There are no limits to options or ideas, so you shouldn't limit yourself in coming up with ideas. Next step: list all the available options you can think of. Initially, just don't nurture the ideas, just list all the options you can think of. After discussing, filter out any ideas that are not possible or are not good ones to try. Then skim the list for ideas that have a high potential of solving your academic homework problem. After filtering it, your next step in the process should be to choose the best option or the option that you believe will work and implement it. Your ultimate goal at the end of the process is to review the results. After choosing and implementing the option, the next step is to review the outcome of what has already been implemented.

One of the most important responsibilities of a parent is to teach children how to deal with problems. This is an important leadership skill. Teachers and parents tend to focus most on academics, but the reality is that we want to raise children who are capable of learning anything. Problem solving is a process. A problem-solving process typically involves the following steps: stating the problem, brainstorming options, choosing and implementing an appropriate solution, reviewing and reflecting on the result. The problem-solving process might seem more lengthy at first, but the more time that is focused on it, the faster the problem gets resolved.

8

Encouraging Empathy and Understanding

To shape your children, to educate them, to teach them by leading them gently, rather than subjecting them in silence: such is the challenge of hieratic paternity. It does not promise that "the child will be civically virtuous and professionally deserving", that "his behavior will always be exemplary". It promises characters capable of loving relationships; that it guarantees the absence of violence. It allows us to find meaning in life and to believe in the future. It is about reacting with intelligence, kindness, always respectful of the person, not his actions. Let us learn to educate our children, but without ever subjecting them. Let us offer family and school atmospheres, if not joyful, at least alive, animated, impartial, open. Where, learning to live, children learn to love. And accept responsibility.

If older siblings become teachers or models for younger ones, everyone benefits. Listen to your feelings and what they are saying instead of banning undesirable behavior. Take advantage of mistakes, transform them into opportunities to do better; often they leave deeper marks than good experiences. On the other hand, avoid - as far as possible - to set traps so that your children make mistakes. And when these happen, remember that you too have sinned. Tell them about your mistake and tell them how you did to rectify it.

Trust yourself, do not be too demanding; give free rein to imagination and animation. Taking charge of a family can be a scary task, and we often confuse firmness with hardness. When violence, as small as it may be, settles at home, how can we hope to evict it? If the atmosphere in the family is suffocating, nothing good can really grow there.

9

Establishing Consistent Consequences

Consistency also means that parents work together to establish guidelines for behavior. These guidelines must be logical and not allow one parent to tolerate or even encourage the punishment of the other parent's children. Once parents have clarity on the guidelines, they must also support each other and show unity to the children. It is easier to be consistent when there is frequent mutual planning. If each parent goes their own way in different situations and disregards the rules or prohibitions set by the other parent, the education and supervision of the children will suffer as a result.

Another important aspect of positive discipline is to strengthen the child's sense of security and self-esteem. It is important to always be loving and firm, but to avoid being overly severe, lenient, indulgent, or permissive. Both strictness and leniency are detrimental when the consequences of behavior are inconsistent, unenforceable, and dependent on the parents' mood. Being predictable empowers children to govern themselves and not rely solely on parental guidance. They can trust that their parents truly believe in the importance of teaching certain behaviors. Predictability also removes the appearance of arbitrary punishment.

10

Building Trust and Communication

Becoming parents is not an easy task. But it is the most valuable investment. A good family is never shown in weaknesses. Family is the bond of love in action. When we are a block and our children feel safe, trust us, and know that we are with them to accompany them and not judge them, they become our best company. You may think that it is impossible to accomplish something like building trust and communication with our offspring following the paradigms that we were educated with and that time still remains and to some extent will continue. But is there anyone who believes that it is "good" to teach lessons that hurt and teach to attack, to compete, to dissuade? I assure you that it is possible and that today there is a purifying wind of enthusiasm in the branches of psychology and pedagogy that deconstruct to reconstruct a new educational measure.

Everyone longs to be loved and trusted. No one wants to be judged, accused, criticized, or blamed for mistakes. It is important to rethink our way of treating our children. Good communication does not consist of ordering, correcting, blaming, threatening, or punishing. Our children are not family servants, points of sale, delinquents, or children who should not be seen or heard. Our children are our best allies. And even if sometimes it gets out of our hands, they never throw in the towel when it comes to looking for a solution.

11

Fostering Independence and Responsibility

If children are disciplined at an early age, they are generally responsible when they are teenagers. If they are not responsible at an early age, they rarely are when they are teenagers. Positive Discipline is more about teaching than changing behavior. Discipline comes from the Latin word 'disciplina' which means teaching, learning, and knowledge. Washing dishes and laundry aren't likely to be seen as annoying chores to an eight-year-old, who has been doing them since they were old enough to stand on a chair and reach the sink or use a stool and reach the knobs on the washer and dryer. Research shows the single best inhibitor to drug use in children is regular participation in family chores. I believe children are better adjusted when they are required to help around the house and are paid less in allowance as a result of having certain responsibilities. Remember, we indulge our children by doing for them what they should be doing for themselves. We spoil them by doing everything we can for them, including what isn't good for them!

To foster independence and responsibility, we need to understand that we can do too much for our children. Indulgence is doing it all for your children and thereby causing them to feel and think that they are entitled to what they don't yet deserve. It is wise to start asking your children to help around the house when they are about two years old. At two years of age, they can learn to pick up their toys when they are finished. I have yet to meet a two-year-old who doesn't like to pick up toys when asked. Soon after two, a child can learn to put away all their toys when they are finished playing. Children as young as three are capable of doing much more. All of mine learned to use our house vacuum cleaner before they were four. They learned this "magic carpet" trick from standing on their mother's feet when she vacuumed.

12

Addressing Challenging Behaviors

In another article, positive parenting that includes positive discipline develops a child's behavior. Michelle McQuaid stated that psychologists John Gottman and Roy Baumeister have shown children who receive positive discipline in a supportive home environment are better students, make better use of their intellectual abilities, and develop personal characteristics that will assist them in becoming a successful adult.

Positive discipline does not mean you should not have any discipline. As researched by Gwen Dewar, Ph.D., psychologist Diana Baumrind has determined that positive discipline is related to helpful behavior, self-control, self-esteem, analytic abilities, and social ability. Negative discipline approaches will limit independence, make children less self-reliant, and make them fearfully dependent.

Encouragement that is led by love and mutual understanding is known as "positive discipline." Positive discipline is focused on taking action as a way of training children. Action can include providing physical, intellectual, and emotional support to assist children in developing their life skills. Instead of simply blocking them from misbehaving, one positive discipline approach is to enable children to understand why their action is in error and encourage them to do the right thing by emphasizing the importance of developing empathy for others and respecting societal rules and regulations.

Although the ultimate goal of discipline is to motivate a child to behave a certain way, there are different approaches to discipline. To some, discipline means punishment, enforcing restrictions, or applying physical force to motivate behavior. In the end, these approaches might lead to a child being compliant or appear more obedient, but that's thanks to fear, not understanding.

13

Promoting Emotional Regulation

Before we begin doing things to help children feel good, it's very important that both children and parents or teachers understand some of these concepts. This can be done simply, yet effectively. Emotional intelligence refers to our ability to understand and manage our feelings in positive ways, to relieve stress, communicate effectively, empathize with others, overcome challenges, and to defuse conflict. Recognizing the signals of feelings makes it possible to manage feelings in a positive way. To teach children how feelings are helpful, we need to believe it ourselves. Since children learn more from what we do than what we say, it's important to remember this every day. Social intelligence includes the skills we need for successful social relationships. Of course, the skills are not straightforward and a list of competencies could include all aspects of social skills. Plenty have been put forth, with slight differences. We're still defining social intelligence, according to Daniel Goleman and others. However, the skills I recommend most for families and classrooms can be reduced to one specific skill: Problem Solving.

Now that we understand how stress interferes with learning and behavior, let's look at some ways to help children create an inner sense of well-being. Learning self-control begins with happy relationship experiences, which start at birth. The interaction between parents and children is what strengthens this vital part of the brain – the basis for self-control, trusting, and empathy. What parents do, specifically, in their interactions with children is what matters most.

14

Nurturing Self-Esteem and Confidence

As much as we could, we should repeatedly and in so many ways possible let our children understand that with or without money, success, and status, one's self-respect and respect of others serve as the best assurance of growth and harmony in the family and, in a radical perspective, in society.

Blaming the child is never a solution; it will only make him feel that the pain he is feeling is a corned beef cramp. On the other hand, too many praises on accomplishments may result in a child who believes that he is somebody very superior to others and so cannot afford to make a mistake. Telling the child that he is smart and beautiful makes him happy, but most of all, confident. In the same way, encourage your children to put on their best and not to look down on others. Tell them that you expect people to take notice of you, so you must give your best in caring for yourself, but more so, in keeping the respect and harmony. Remind them to strive to be worthy of the respect of others.

When reminding the children of their wrongdoings, it is vital to help them understand the consequences/negative effects that could happen when someone, looking at the event from another perspective, may find comfort and contentment at the expense of others.

After the child acknowledges his wrong and promises not to do it again, hug and assure him that the ironed-out incident serves as a guide for the future. It is also far more beneficial for the child if we give him the chance to make the changes on his own without our intervention.

Now comes the most tricky part of this approach, but also very beneficial for the child. It is very easy for a child to develop an inferiority complex or, on another extreme, a superiority complex. Through positive and loving discipline, it primarily teaches the children the important values in life: respect toward one another, understanding for the needs of others, and most of all, to learn from every opportunity, to take heartaches, shame, and disappointments as challenges, not as dreadful and frustrating experiences.

15

Supporting Social Skills Development

From infancy to adolescence, the following are particularly important skills parents can develop in their children: - Recognizing the feelings of others. - Taking turns during social interactions. - Listening (and talking) during conversations. - Respecting the personal space of others. - Recognizing and solving social problems during interaction. - Preserving friendships (some connections will of course be stronger than others). - Showing empathy and compassion. - Seeking help when needed. - Valuing social customs, rules, and culture. - Identifying unjust or unfair behavior and knowing how to respond.

Encouraging children to learn lots of words and to use language in all sorts of ways sets the stage for a lifetime of successful communication. There are also basic communication skills that facilitate the ability to interact with others and to form lasting personal connections. As the child grows, she needs lots of interpersonal practice to develop the social skills necessary to use language effectively. Personal interactions require a unique set of skills children can develop with the help of adults who understand how human relationships work. Parents can play a significant role in ensuring the child is socially adept.

16

Strengthening the Parent-Child Relationship

One of the most difficult aspects of parenting is finding effective, yet non-punitive ways, to discipline children. While you may need to use various behavior modification programs or other discipline strategies, ideally the experiences you share with your child provide most of the discipline. These instructions presented by my mom and various addendums from my own experiences are provided as a framework and a reminder that no matter how old your child is, maintaining the parental relationship is the first priority of successful discipline. Remember the negative mental health effects felt during adolescence in Jon McKnight's "risky behaviors" section (P:315)? These health results show the importance of parental influence during challenging times. Positive discipline helps maintain this relationship, especially during difficult times, by avoiding the causes of negative relationships presented in McKnight's book.

Just as positive discipline reinforces the teacher-student relationship and the social contract of a learning community, it also works to strengthen the parent-child relationship. In our hurried lives, it's extremely difficult to keep the relationship a priority. When we feel under the gun, we all tend to revert to an "I'm-the-parent-and-I-say-so" type of attitude. Sometimes kids need to listen to us just because they do! But when we rely on this strategy too much, it damages relationships and reduces influence. I learned a few years ago, through a child-raising lecturer, that children must feel a solid connection to their parents to become people who care what their parents think. Kate's comment that good relationships are a prime requirement to influence is also true for business relationships, student-teacher relationships, and ourselves as members of our community. To be present for the relationship, we require an understanding and commitment to maintaining a positive relationship so we do not inadvertently strain it.

17

Collaborating with Teachers and Caregivers

This begins with trust building. Help build a sense of trust between your child and his or her teacher. When children feel that teachers are effective at keeping them emotionally safe, they begin to feel safe so that they can take on the risks that accompany the learning process. Teachers at cooperative preschools believe that the first socializing unit is the family. During this time, children learn values through the guidance and reinforcement of their family community. The family teaches children trust, respect, love, physical care, humanitarianism, emotional sensitivity, and the absorption of a shared vision and commitment.

One of the most important times to help your child feel successful is when they are at school. If a child continues to feel failure at their place of education, it can lead to self-doubt and a reluctance to approach certain subject matters or classes. They can become preoccupied with the need to fit in socially with their peers, as well as academically with the standards and expectations of their teachers. All of this can lead to shortened attention spans, difficulties in following through with tasks to completion, and issues with self-motivation.

When a child attends a preschool, it is important to work with your child's teacher in coordinating your efforts on following through with positive discipline from the school to your home. Children need consistent rules and expectations across their environments, which will make them feel more secure. By working with their teachers, together you can create a caring partnership that will be instrumental in teaching children the self-discipline they need in order to be successful.

18

Handling Sibling Conflicts

Creating such a win-win solution is important. If children themselves solve the problem, they will more willingly comply with the decision. But be ready to step in when the decision making reaches nowhere and the fight becomes overpowering. Team building activities are important so that children bond with each other. Playing, working on a similar ground such as gardening, or coloring or cleaning the shelves together will do a lot of good. So is having common rules. When siblings see parents following the same rules with each other and with them, they are more likely to follow the given rules. For instance, suppose the rule is 'No TV while eating' but one day children see their mother munching on her evening snack as she watches the TV, they'll question her integrity in obeying rules, without knowing she let them watch TV during mealtime while they were napping. Therefore, parents need to be good examples of what they want their children to become. After all, becoming a good person starts at home.

Sibling conflicts will be there, but as adults, we need to show children how to handle it in a mature manner. Effective communication can help children see each other's point of view. With older children, you can help them come up with a solution that everyone agrees with. Coming up with rules that are fair to all parties is an important step in problem-solving. For example, for children fighting over the TV remote control, a mother can create a schedule. Tony can watch TV from 5 PM to 6 PM and Terry gets her time from 6:30 PM to 7:30 PM, and so on.

19

Promoting Healthy Boundaries

More to the point, aside from fostering and employing empathy, kindness, love, and respect in accurate and frequent doses – not too much, not too little – another proven method for promoting healthy boundaries as a discipline tool is the use of Positive Discipline – a technique of communicating head-on with your child via your own actions, words, and body language to manage the child in effect, not merely his behavior.

One way how children know and understand what respect and dignity imply is by the way they and others are treated. A parent who demonstrates kindness, understanding, support, and empathy towards her child teaches her child values of empathy, compassion, strength, and understanding. Thus, in time, children grow to understand and develop the kind of patience, kindness, understanding, and respect that they, in turn, were shown and experienced firsthand in their early development.

First of all, it is important to point out that healthy boundaries do not spring forth out of thin air, out of a vacuum, and most definitely not out of the clear, blue sky. Boundaries are slowly and painstakingly crafted early in childhood, established through attention, reinforcement, and observation. Another way children learn and interpret the concept of boundaries is through the parents themselves, who are the first point of reference in their lives.

Healthy boundaries are crucial in the dynamics of any given relationship, and this rule applies as much for the relationship between parent and child as it does for the connection between family members. However, it is also true that quite often many individuals take for granted the configuration of what boundaries must be inherent in any interaction, as well as what the appropriate way to handle said limits in a healthy, respectful way could entail.

20

Addressing Bullying and Peer Pressure

Peer Pressure Parents are often quite alarmed by the lack of judgment they perceive in their adolescent following the input from friends. In a study with instant response clicker units, teens realized with great swiftness and alacrity that their chances of success in a jello-eating contest were actually very low simply by observing the actions of the friends alongside them. In a similar experiment, the willingness of adolescents to give an obviously wrong answer to simple math questions, joining in with others who provided the error, was almost double that evidenced by the twenties and thirties age group. A study simulating the influence of college roommates on adult drinking behavior found that an adult who drinks the equivalent of two beers nightly would consume almost three per night with the influence of the roommate. Another study comparing mock jury selection by groups of erstwhile college friends with groups of random volunteers unveiled a chance of 40% of the latter choice being reversed if members of the group were informed of the individual results of their private conferring. While group members influenced one another with 100% unanimity, this difference could be brought out when individuals felt secure in their own decisions and able to voice them.

Bullying Early in their lives, children are somewhat aggressive. When a baby is frustrated, the only means of communication is crying. Later, when the baby starts to move, more sophisticated tactics for gaining the parent's attention can be used, such as grabbing objects, pushing, and occasionally biting. The toddler may become jealous of the affection shown to a new sibling or become possessive of toys. This ingrained nature is not the same as the aggressive behavior labeled bullying, which is deliberate hurtful behaviors repeated over time. Decades ago, the classic bullying scenario revolved around the big, strong kid taunting or physically overpowering the smaller child, and early generations often told themselves that the experience would "toughen up" the smaller child, building character for facing multitudes of bigger, stronger, and more authoritative tormentors in later life. It was an attitude in which strength, authority, and superior age were accorded greater rights and privileges, where a child was told to stick up for themselves in order to "toughen up," "fight back," or "give it to them." Seldom did this advice prevent the child from hating to go to school or from losing faith and trust in a caring adult who gave ineffective advice. In recent years, through cases of tragic results, this behavior has been brought to the forefront, and scenarios reflecting bullying have expanded to include non-physical, cyber, and environmental, or "eco-bullying" aspects.

21

Managing Technology Use

Situational awareness for personal security while absent from the supportive adult are elements which responsible parents of all ages know intuitively using their life experiences. Naturally, parents do this intuitively requiring the children to provide ample means of communication mechanisms within the physical world in addition to the presented method of reaching out to the supported adult. Integrating the same elements into the digital world so that the parent supporting the non-developed thinking adult can prepare for emergent chats to resolve the issue using the same thought process found in Unified Communications would follow much the same process flow.

To those under the umbrella of digital safety and digital wellness for the family, everyone must telescope their situational awareness to the way people are communicating with others, how they are interconnecting with others and be able to understand the communication being used to avoid what the National Center for Missing & Exploited Children alludes to as a possible cyber tip. The responsible parent regardless of the absences within an appropriately constructed code base for technology use within the family, will also investigate to gather the leaking Digital DNA data by using reconnaissance through some other mechanisms as well. Family members should be well informed of security alerts and should take appropriate steps to patch or correct the situation.

The creative uses of technology designed for productivity can bring enormous benefits to individuals, families, and society. Technology can also be a hindrance and create a multitude of social issues. While advancements in technology can bring undeniable improvements to our society, it is the relationships people have with others where technology tends to disrupt the natural flow of discipline inherent. Routine activities around technologies when not mitigated utilizing the same work ethics as would be when not using technology, data privacy issues, and data security concerns associated with using and managing technology need much of the same strategic thought as does budget planning and industrial espionage protection to bring to light the little things that can have detrimental outcomes within a controlled environment.

22

Teaching Respect and Kindness

Another way to model respectful and kind behavior is to make sure you include your children in your communication and decision-making process. I am not suggesting that children and adults should make the decisions together. I am suggesting that we know what our children think and feel. We do listen to their ideas and feelings. We don't put them down or say something that sounds like they are being ridiculous. They can share their opinions without being judged, just as we can with them. "Use kind and firm words, demonstrating respect" too. Kind and firm words, two vital words when incorporating the positive discipline model, which is "kind" to engender respect and "firm" to promote self-discipline. Always tell your children that love is unconditional. Allow your children to give input and ask their opinions when possible. Implement family meetings and private time to foster family interaction and self-reflection. Building a close relationship with your child...it is caring, respect, kindness, humor, empathy, patience, competence, wisdom, love, and consistent self-exploration, that all contribute to building a lasting friendship with your child.

How can we use the eleven positive discipline principles to teach and encourage respectful and kind behavior? Begin by being respectful and kind yourself. Also, model these behaviors toward your children and toward others. Your children are watching. They are much more likely to repeat what you do than what you say. Try not to have the attitude that "no one is perfect" when you make the same mistakes over and over. What does this attitude really teach? I think it can sometimes teach that self-growth is not what is the most important. As I mention this, should I add not to have respect for yourself? Of course not. Yes, we do need to accept and be kind to ourselves, in my opinion. But maybe we need to balance that with a fair amount of "I want to grow, to try to change and be better."

23

Encouraging Mindfulness and Self-Reflection

We provide to help reflect this existence on those values: Sometimes you can find a beautiful terrace, where you can see wonderful flowers sway, but somehow you hear silence. So ask: "Why is it silent?" They will answer you: "We welcome you through an action free from noise." And they force you to appreciate the silent flowering. Peace and calm, it is inconvenient, a teaching of silence. A good operation when action becomes silent, an operation that requires the investment of methodologies. Sometimes, you can find a beautiful terrace, where you can see wonderful flowers sway, but somehow you feel the silence. In the Montessori Methodology, silence is a matter of good operation in good training, and an operation that is silent can lead to the development of wisdom virtues such as mindfulness and self-reflection.

Mindfulness and the practice of self-reflection, responsiveness and caregiving attention to each child, are identified as wisdom virtues which help to develop the so-called executive functioning that science attributes to specific centers in the human brain. This no longer deals, as during the so-called psychosexual phase, with communicative functions, the search for words, the exchange of information. It is the cerebral capacity that will allow children to be able to face more adult tasks. In the human being, the capacity of planning, focused attention, social relations, or action plans they found, then the emotion-regulating systems necessary to learn complex behaviors. It's good for everyone to be aware of the incredible value of these two virtues, as it enables parents to better understand what the children in the family.

How do you encourage mindfulness and self-reflection during interactions with young people? These virtues are of primary importance in the process of personality development from toddlerhood. They give children the key to understanding everything else, fostering an ability to learn, to be a person of good. This isn't a simple task. One needs to keep the foundational consoles of parental subjects, guiding children to better intentions, preventing them from straying off the road to goodness or disrespecting family values. Among the experts in the field of pedagogy, dedicated to children, families, and the relationship between them, Maria Montessori is considered an eminent figure.

24

Dealing with Tantrums and Meltdowns

Something to emphasize right from the start is that pressure ushers in resistance. This doesn't work only for boys, although everyone seems to keep trying to make them work with pressure. This also works with babies, any animal, and even plants! So the more anxious you get about the meltdown or the tantrum, the worse those things get. The calmer you are, the faster the nervous system of your child is going to be able to connect back and function normally. If it's possible, you have to detach yourself from their feeling. You really detach when you give up on telling the child that it's going to be okay. Detach also means helping the child feel safe by giving over and over again the same message, and then just being in the place of calm and love. The most counter-intuitive part of this process is deciding to do nothing about their misbehavior. When your child is having a tantrum, you have to see the feelings that he or she is displaying as very real and legitimate—even though they are not reliable. You, as the safe adult, have to take all feelings seriously. If your kids were at preschool and someone punched them in the arm, how would you handle that? You'd take it very seriously. Discuss it and try to deal with it. When your child is going berserk, you need to take that very seriously, too. Children cannot totally control their behavior; but they always control their feelings. A child's defenses are up the minute he or she senses that someone is trying to control her feelings.

Is there anyone today who doesn't have some kind of anxiety disorder or personality disorder? Most of the ones I see come from tantrums and meltdowns in childhood, compounded by punishment and reward systems. Most of the adults are dealing with unresolved issues from their childhood that have left them in a constantly reactive, self-absorbed, and very, very unhappy states. So it's very important to know how to handle tantrums and meltdowns lovingly when they come. Let's look at the difference: A tantrum comes from defiance—"I won't do it" or "I don't want to do it." A meltdown comes from an overwhelming feeling. Children don't have the capacity to deal with those feelings, so they just melt down. They don't have the words to say, "I'm very tired" or "I'm overwhelmed." The nervous system just shuts down. A tantrum or a meltdown is not something children do in creation; something caused it.

25

Building Resilience and Coping Skills

People learn from mistakes and much can be learned from an honest parent's admission of mistakes. Consider occasionally sharing some of the problems you experienced at their age. If necessary, write a note indicating you overreacted and why that was wrong. Subsequently, in an open manner and depending on the child's age, confess to the child without giving justifications of anger and self-centered. Older children will appreciate that you respect them because you dared to admit your fears and faults. This can also be a wonderful opportunity for a reflective discussion, during which you can ask your child to differentiate between "forgive me" and "give permission." It is important to remember that discipline shake-ups can cause shock and suppress initial resilience. Work together to remove all innocent people from the room where the problem arose. When the time is right, demonstrate responsible, positive, and disciplined behavior. Afterward, debrief the situation with honest feedback.

When we speak about fostered resilience, we are describing the ability to bounce back from adversity. Parents can directly build resilience by using positive discipline. On the contrary, shame-based discipline can damage resilience. In their painful and confusing world, children can as easily become abusive towards themselves as they can towards others, with long and painful effects. A parent's aim should be to help him/her feel accepted and loved. Do not let your shame or your embarrassment lead you to put the primary emphasis on earning your child's future approval in the moment.

26

Recognizing and Encouraging Effort

It is also the first letter of each of the eight principles in Positive Discipline. Be kind. Show faith in your child. In a difficult situation, you might not feel that your child is capable of "x." So you, rather than your child, approach the task with an assumption of incompetence. Assuming incompetence gives the wrong message and can result in your child living up to our unspoken assumptions. We believe the greatest gift you can give your child is the transfer of adult confidence. Far better to quietly teach or model a skill than to make it known that you think your child is incapable. Find something positive to recognize. Encouragement is not a technique. When we have genuine faith, we will look for the good to recognize. Making an effort is nothing to downplay. Meanwhile, saying something like "You gave it a try" would honor the courage involved. The beauty of recognizing, rather than praising greatness and effort, is that we can be sincere and not turn everything into a sugar-coated spoonful of nothing.

Effective discipline is mutual respect. It is not about us, the adults, being in charge or about power. Most people think of "discipline" as punishment. Discipline simply teaches. It teaches children how to behave, what to believe about themselves, and how to make good decisions that grow into good behavior. For discipline to work effectively, adults need to be nurturing and kind, yet firm with high standards and expectations. This is also known as "authoritative," respectful, and positive discipline. In harmony. It takes so much love for your child to guide their behavior proactively.

27

Balancing Discipline and Freedom

Children also need freedom. As you consider drawing guidelines and boundaries, remember to balance children's need for self-control with their need for enough freedom to make reasonable decisions to demonstrate their self-control. Guidelines, boundaries, rules, and limits that are too severe, stifling, and suppressive can negatively impact a child's journey toward self-discipline. Provide children with generous space to explore and experiment and plenty of opportunities to make their choices. One of the gifts a parent has the option of offering to a child is the freedom to choose his actions: a human right, a basic need. Invite your child to sometimes choose among alternatives you think are acceptable. With parental support, children should experience the natural, occasionally painful consequences of their decisions about expending their resources, understanding that they ultimately control an incredible power within themselves, a power to govern their own behavior. This is not to say parents should take a completely hands-off approach to guiding the course of their children's behavior. On the contrary, effective discipline involves a balance of restrictions and freedoms. Awareness of the importance of this balance can help in striking it successfully.

Children need discipline: guidelines, boundaries, rules, and limits to help them feel secure. Although discipline can, from time to time, appear punitive, authentic discipline is not punishment. It is consistent, firm guidance to help a child gain self-discipline. Through responsibly teaching and verbally coaching our children about ethical standards, morality, and responsibilities, we help them make competent decisions, which will help them forge relationships built on genuine respect.

28

Addressing Specific Age-Related Challenges

In this section, we discuss common age-related challenges and explore how parents might respond positively to them: - Toddlers: Threes are usually struggling between needing to master an increasingly complex world and mastering the skills necessary to overcome the anger, persecution, and frustration of trying to achieve independence. This attempt to gain some personal independence can manifest itself in an increased desire to declare "no," goodwill, resistance, anger, embarrassment, or defiance. - Preschoolers: Children at this age tend to be very eager to learn about and act well. This desire can lead to cooperation, collaboration, and willingness to comply with the rules in family life. - School Years: School-age children can convince themselves that others are thinking of them, assessing them, and being negatively critical of them, and that they have been noticed, understood, and agreed upon. These and others can lead to exaggerated responses and behavior. - Adolescents: Adolescents tend to choose themselves as individuals. They are usually in love with teamwork partners but are typically torn between wishing to belong to the community and becoming slaves to the power of the group.

Positive Discipline is more than just a set of techniques to help manage your child. It is a comprehensive system that is founded on the belief that healthy family communication and closeness is possible and that, with intentional effort, families can be complete while providing their children with the kind of firm, loving, and respectful foundation they need to flourish. Whether your child is a toddler or a teen, Positive Discipline is an amazing system for maintaining order in the home, while fostering learning, independence, responsibility, and love. It works because it gives kids consistent and clear parental responses to their behaviors, and, at the same time, fosters respect, mutual cooperation, joy, and wonderful family connections.

29

Cultivating a Growth Mindset

When we might be choosing to take action on the belief that intelligence and abilities can be changed in our children, we are focused on the present moment and on their children's progress, more than on their success or failure. When they problem-solve, children need to focus on the problem at hand and find a solution. When we make our children aware of how much effort they put into something, we are informing them that the more effort they put into it, the better the outcome. Uncertain about the quality and value of his ideas, Peter (3 years old) hesitates to participate in conversations and struggles when he encounters a task that is a little more difficult. Concerned about his self-esteem and progress, his mother ensures that Peter finds opportunities to problem-solve by avoiding offering the solutions himself and openly acknowledging the strategies, effort, and abilities that the child uses to produce an acceptable result.

What is a growth mindset? Our beliefs influence how we feel and what we do. If we believe that our intelligence, ability, and talent can be developed, we are said to have what is called a "growth mindset". If we believe that intelligence, ability, and talent cannot be changed, we are said to have a "fixed mindset". A growth mindset leads to resilience, understanding struggle as an integral part of learning, and being persistent in the face of challenges. People with a fixed mindset will feel helpless, and when they face difficulties, they may think that they are not smart (or good at something) and, hence, are not able to do anything about it. Positive Discipline practices target the development of a growth mindset in the children to help them acquire a sense of responsibility for learning, even in times of trouble.

30

Emphasizing Positive Role Models

Good role modeling is an extremely effective means for shaping behavior as your kids grow. We all know that you model behavior when you ask your children to be quiet at the movie theater and when you ask them to share their toys with friends. However, you also model behavior every time you are a consumer, every time you are a friend, your life partner, when you face stress, or even when you are polite with strangers. For example, think about how you act when there is a traffic jam. You model to your kids whether you remain patient when there is nothing you can do or when you maintain a courteous and respectful manner.

Effective parenting features positive role models for kids to follow, and it is based on the idea that a large part of a child's learning is done through unconditional respect and love, as well as the physical and emotional support from the family. By showing respect and love for your family, you can teach your kids about positive relationships based on trust. This approach to discipline emphasizes good models for your kids, and it is based on the idea that a large part of a child's learning is through the unconditional respect and love that families pour out for their kids, as well as the physical and emotional support those families provide.

31

Celebrating Achievements and Progress

Celebrations state and describe what the child did that is being praised. Use of the word "I" refers to the child rather than the adult. "You prepared a very beautiful message in braille on your slate. I'm proud of you" is an example. Avoid rewards that amount to bribes or that forecast deprivation. Instead of awards or stickers display kindness and show appreciation for effort and progress: "I appreciate that you are practicing writing. The letter is taking shape. You understand how to represent sounds with letters." Discipline as punishment is confusion. So is the introduction of external rewards to replace autonomy and intrinsic motivation. Time-oriented rewards, tangible gifts, conditional parental love, indicates that the parent does not have faith that the child is able to self-discipline with respect to effort and exploration. The following quote from Zhēn Figueras, a classroom teacher and Positive Discipline Associate in Costa Rica, exemplifies meaningful celebrations.

Meaningful celebrations focus on the child's accomplishment and how it reflects progress rather than innate talent. Parental comments explicitly attribute the child's success to specific effort, strategy, and other evidence of self-discipline. Celebrations aim to maintain and enhance motivation, not to deflect it to other activities or to relatives. They avoid conveying that the person being rewarded is you. Positive reinforcing feedback is honest and sincere. It is appropriate to commemorate improvement and progress. It includes a description of what was accomplished and praise for the process used to obtain a goal: "Pablo's sister didn't have a positive attitude when she started school, either. But now she's very happy with herself. It is great that you are enjoying yourself too. Studying can help you learn, like it's helping her. It is true that the words of The Little Engine that Could are very wise," Grace's grandmother commented, expressing a growth mindset.

32 Conclusion

Children's education is a challenge for all the agents that participate in the creation of values and attitudes. When it comes to parenting, the task becomes more complicated as it should stimulate the development of their personality, their independence, and their social relationships. It is also necessary to establish rules so that life at home is harmonious. Parents want their children to grow up strong and happy, and to be adaptable citizens who know how to face life with intelligence and self-esteem. And, to achieve this, discipline is an important educational tool because it allows us to transmit the limits in a loving way, helping to satisfy the need of the child in search for safety and autonomy.

Using positive discipline strategies from a very young age can help parents and teachers develop strong, healthy communicative relationships with children and encourage them to overcome problems. In this way, it would help to reduce the number of children attending psycho-pedagogical centers for having behavior problems, as well as those who are abandoned in foster homes, since fostering the transmission of values and skills to manage frustrating situations positively helps that children who learn to manage their conflicts positively with one another.

Printed by Libri Plureos GmbH in Hamburg,
Germany